Mel B

Don't Be Scared

The author and publishers have made every reasonable effort to contact all copyright holders. Any errors that may have occurred are inadvertent and anyone who for any reason has not been contacted is invited to write to the publishers so that a full acknowledgement may be made in subsequent editions of this work.

This book is sold subject to the condition that it shall not by way of trade or otherwise be lent, resold, hired or otherwise circulated without the prior written consent of the Spice Girls in any form other than that which it has been published.

Research
Noam Friedlander

Design
JMP Ltd

Photography
The Spice Girls' families
Ray Burmiston
Chris Buck
Rankin Waddell
Alex Bailey
Adrian Green
Michael Ginsberg

Copyright © Spice Girls Ltd 1997.
All rights reserved.
All photographs reproduced by kind permission of The Spice Girls.

The right of the Spice Girls to be identified as the authors of this book has been asserted by them in accordance with the Copyright, Designs and Patents Act 1988.

Second edition
First published in 1997 by
Zone/Chameleon Books
an imprint of Andre Deutsch Ltd.
a member of the VCI plc Group
106 Great Russell Street
London WC1B 3LJ
in association with 19 Management Ltd
Printed in Italy by G. Canale & C. Turin

Spice Girls Management
Simon Fuller @ 19 Management

Thanks to
Catri Drummond
James Freedman
Sally Hudson
Gerrard Tyrrell

CIP Data for this title is available from the British Library

A Zone production

ISBN 0223 99323 1

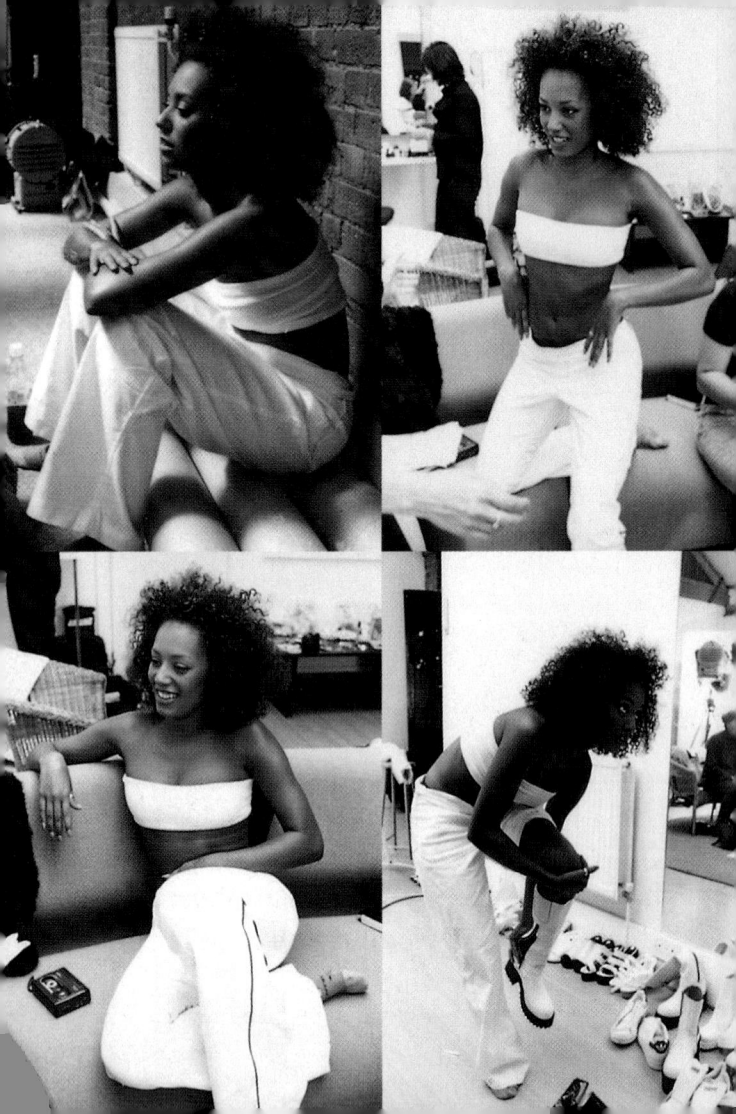

"If you want to speak up, speak up and don't be afraid to do it. Never shut yourself up — if you feel the instinctive urge to scream or say something, then do it!"

"I hate organisation in life. I want chaos and spur-of-the-moment action. I'm impulsive, strong-willed and try and live life to the max."

"You should wear whatever you want to wear. I think it's rubbish when people say you shouldn't wear red if you've got red hair. Apparently, if you look into the pupils of your eyes you can see the colour that's supposed to suit you."

"He's very nice and he took time out for everyone. He's got a great voice and he's very pleasant. No matter who you were he'd speak to you like a lady. I like him."

"This is Spicespot, I call him Spot, because he's got spots all over his body, tail and head. He's also got webbed feet, like a lizard — he's beautiful. Way back his ancestors were bred with leopards and tigers."

"Coming from Leeds makes me feel grounded in this mad life so big-up my Leeds crew. You know who you are!"

"I like honesty and a good time."

"I'm at peace with the way I am and I want to experience as much as possible."

"My way of relaxing is to meditate in my meditation chair. It's really low and you sit down cross-legged in it — I find it very calming."

"You can get by confidence back by pampering yourself, being good to your body and good to yourself when you look in the mirror — smile, don't say yeuch! Accept yourself and make the most of things."

"Girl Power is a vibe, a feeling of liberation and the freedom to be whatever you like."

"I don't do quiet!"

"The most Girl Powerful thing I do is to tell people what I think about them. I'm really honest about it and say what I feel. I just get frustrated that people aren't more real and genuine with each other and never get straight to the point. I'd prefer someone to tell me the way I'd tell them, rather than be talked about or whispered about behind my back."

"I'd like to go completely Indian. I like that cultural stuff, like Afro-Caribbean, when they wear a big turban and traditional dress. I love dresssing up like that."

"I've got Girl Power because I appreciate that I'm mixed race and I follow my own roots."

"From the age of fourteen, I've always said what I think, whether it's got me into trouble or not. I can't help expressing my opinion, I'm very straight and direct."

"Smells are like music — they remind you of so many different things — old aftershave, the smell of your mum's washing."

"I still think Geri's a nutter. She hasn't changed!"

"HELP" vs in KOREA!!

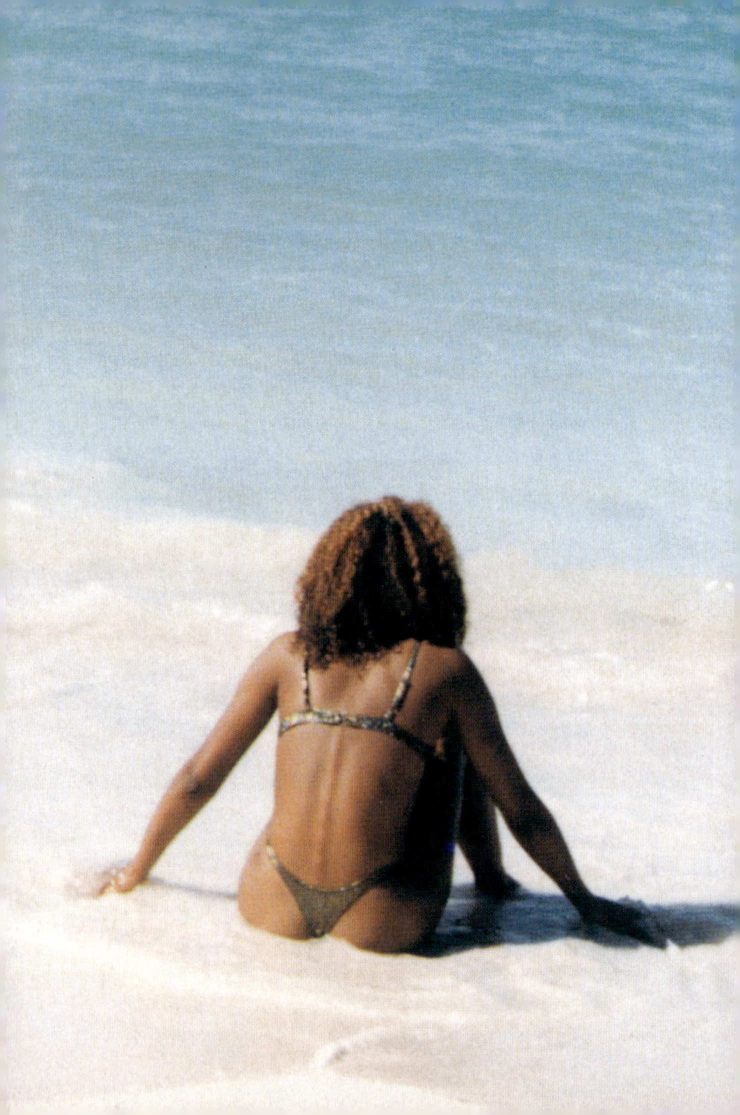

"I try and envision a white light around everyone and I say to myself. 'I love myself and everyone around me,' about 20 times, breathing slowly. And then what I'm thinking about goes away and I begin chilling out. I didn't learn it anywhere – I'm sure it's not proper meditation but it's what I do to relax. Taking your mind off problems helps you put things in perspective. I find my head's much clearer afterwards."

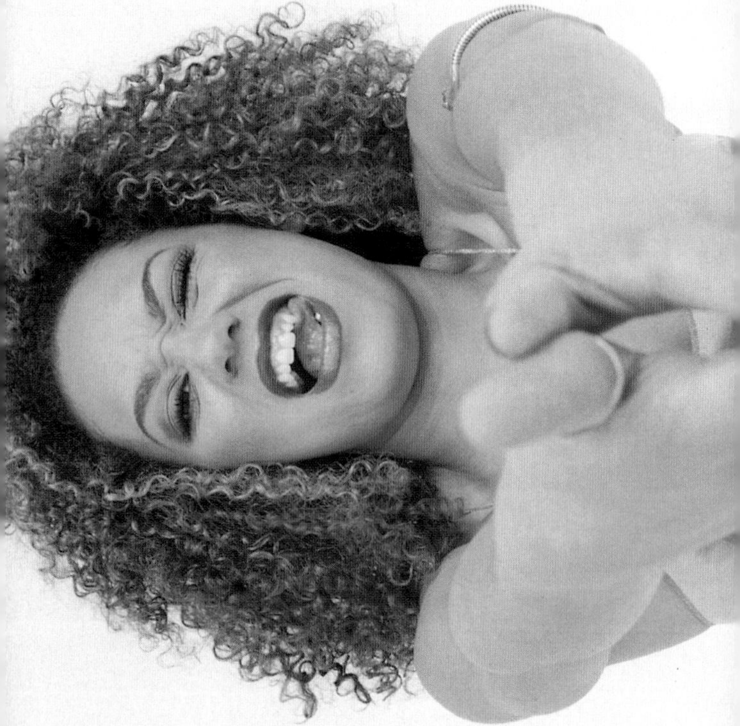

"My worst habit is definitely playing with my tongue ring – I've actually chipped my tooth doing it – and I used to bite my toenails."

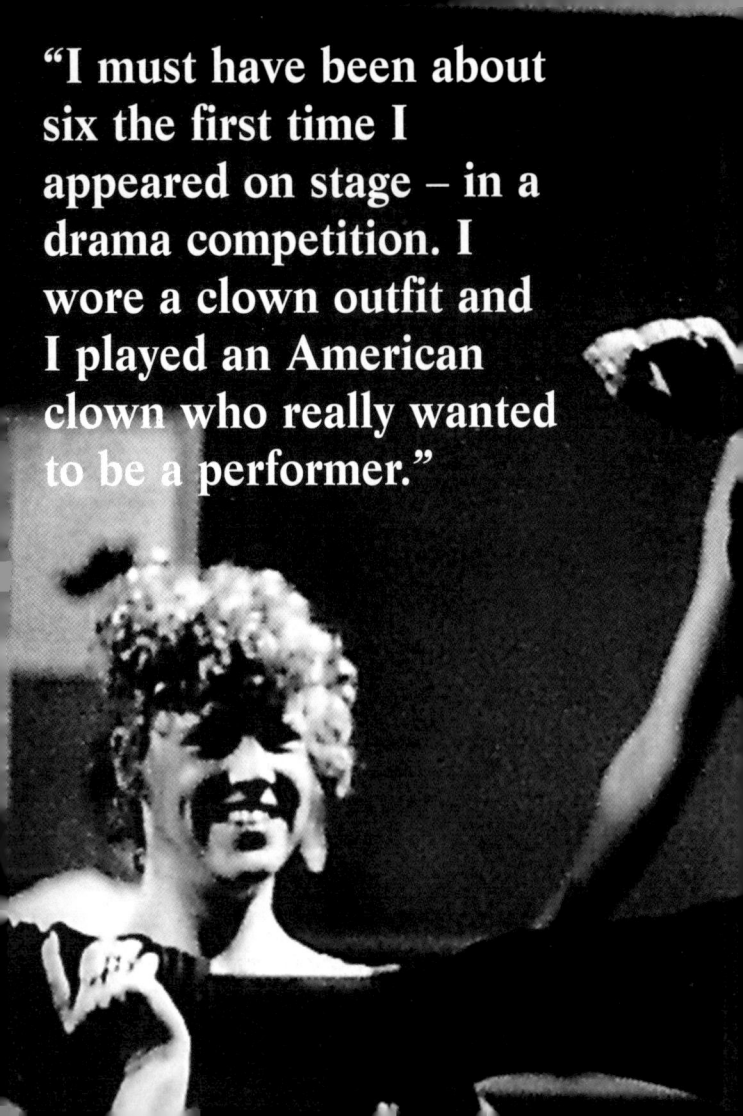

"I must have been about six the first time I appeared on stage – in a drama competition. I wore a clown outfit and I played an American clown who really wanted to be a performer."

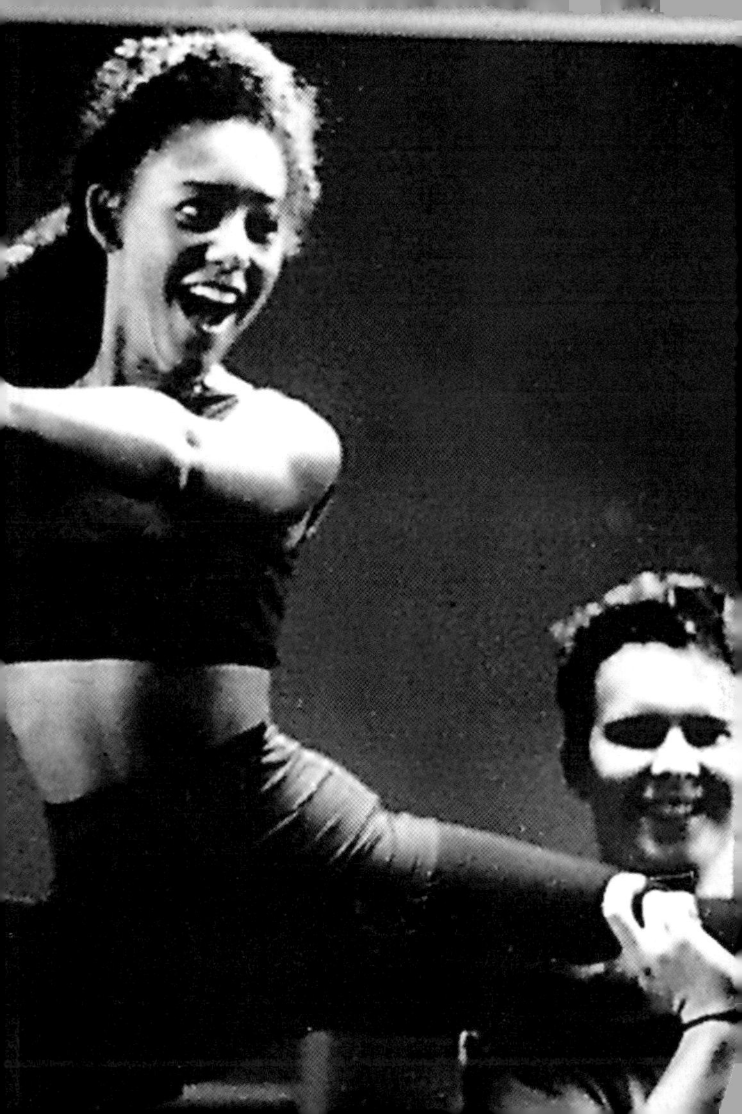

"Do have confidence, but don't use it in the wrong way by being too full of yourself. You shouldn't feel like you have to prove anything to anybody else."

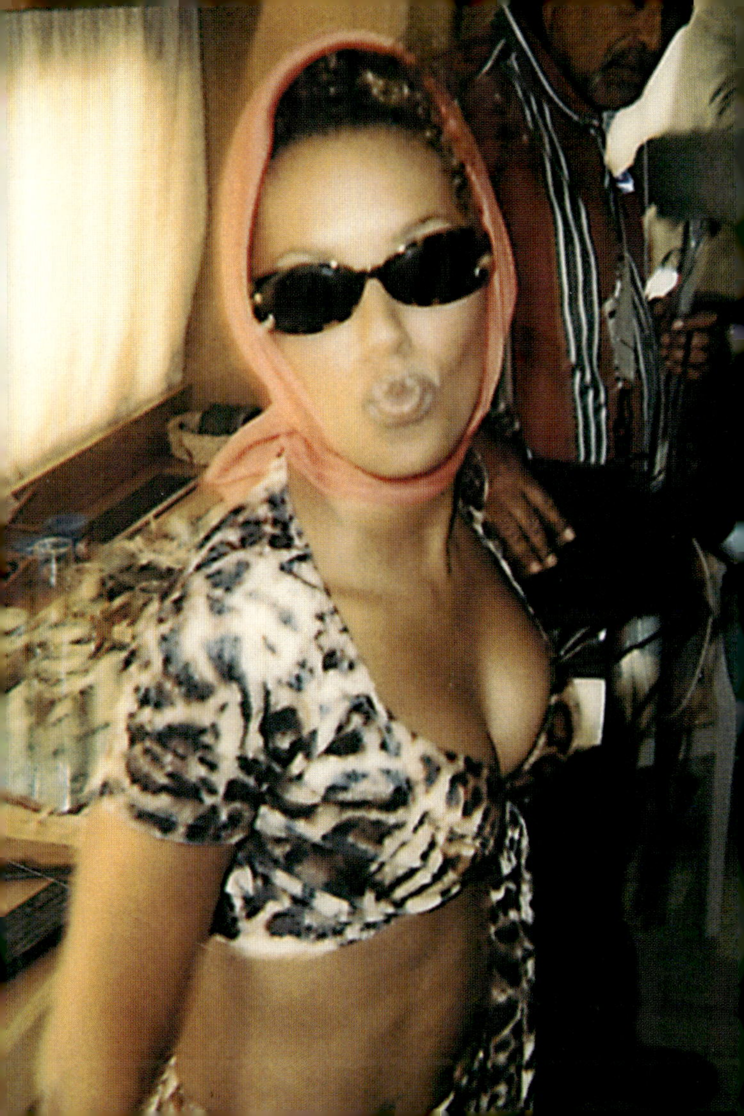

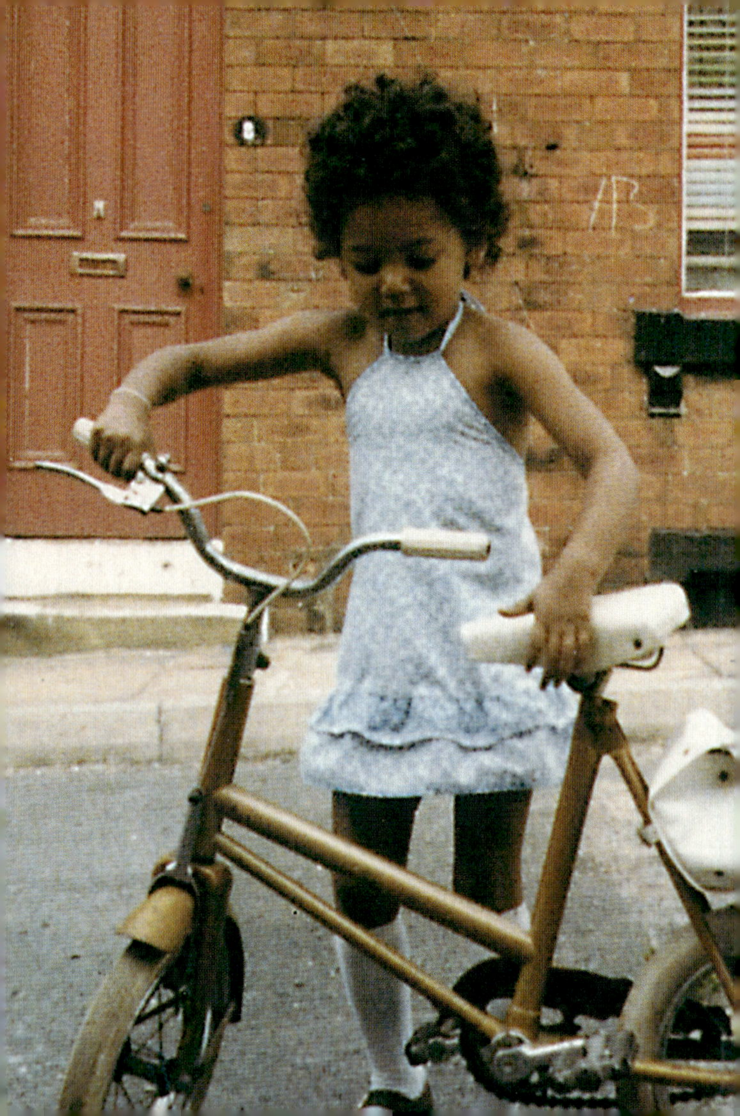

"I think that life, living, sorting yourself out and getting out there is the greatest education you can ever have."

"I hate negativity, jealousy and racism."

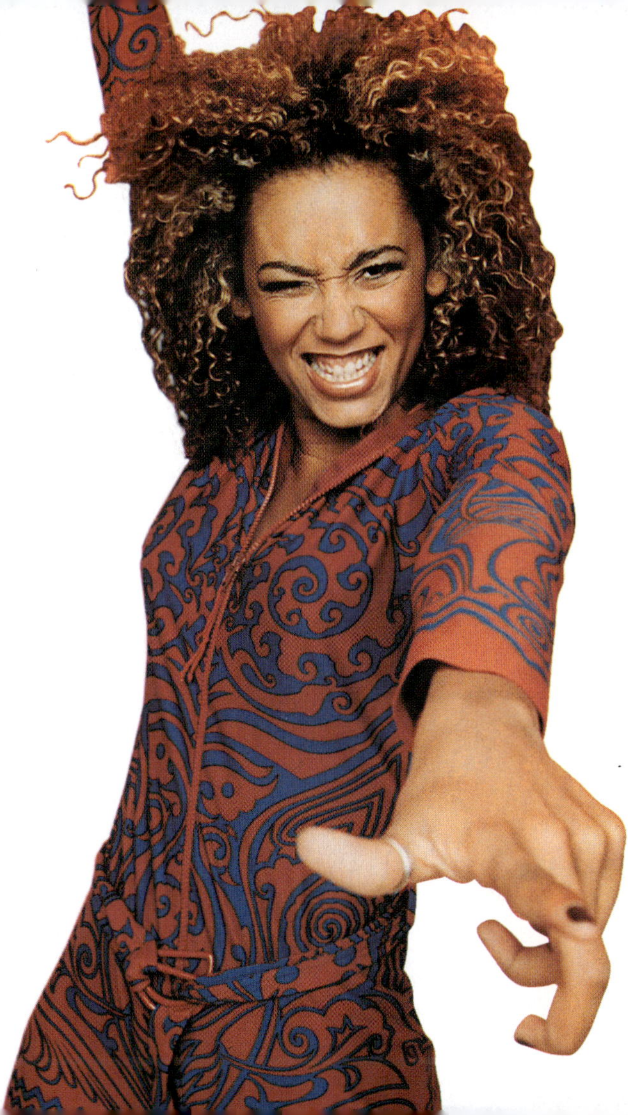

"I think I've changed since we've become successful – I get highs and I get lows and I'm never constantly on one level anymore."

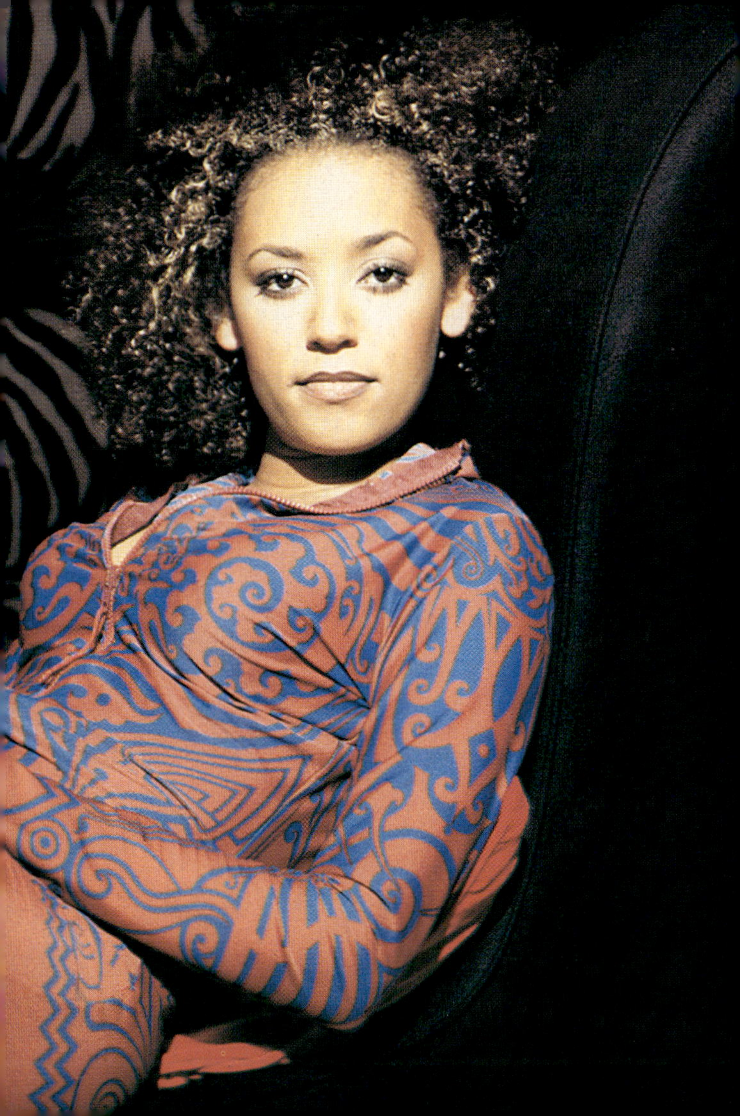

"Every girl's got a right

to stick up for herself."

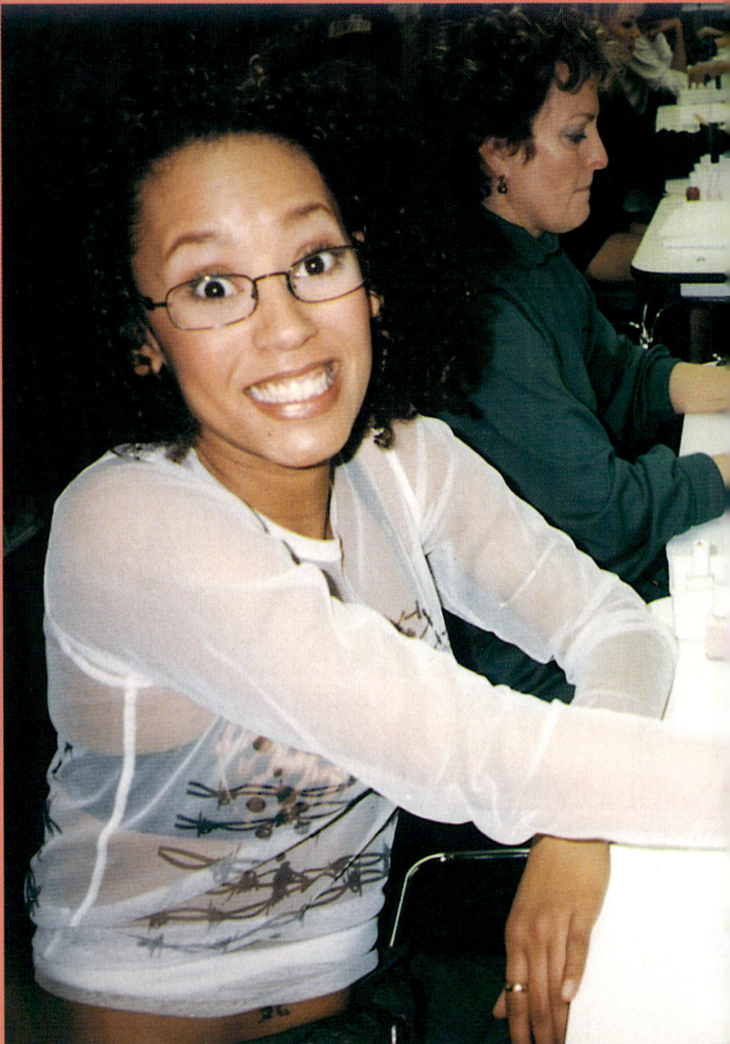

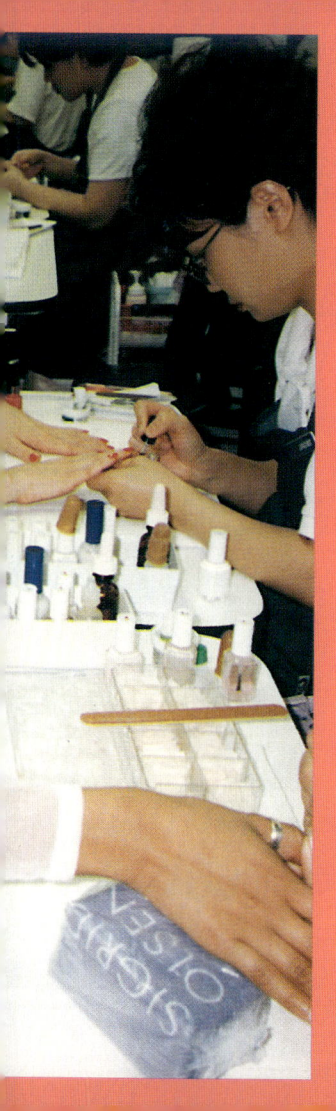

"Being normal and being thrown into such a bizarre world is a perfect combination. I just hope I can cling on to that normality."

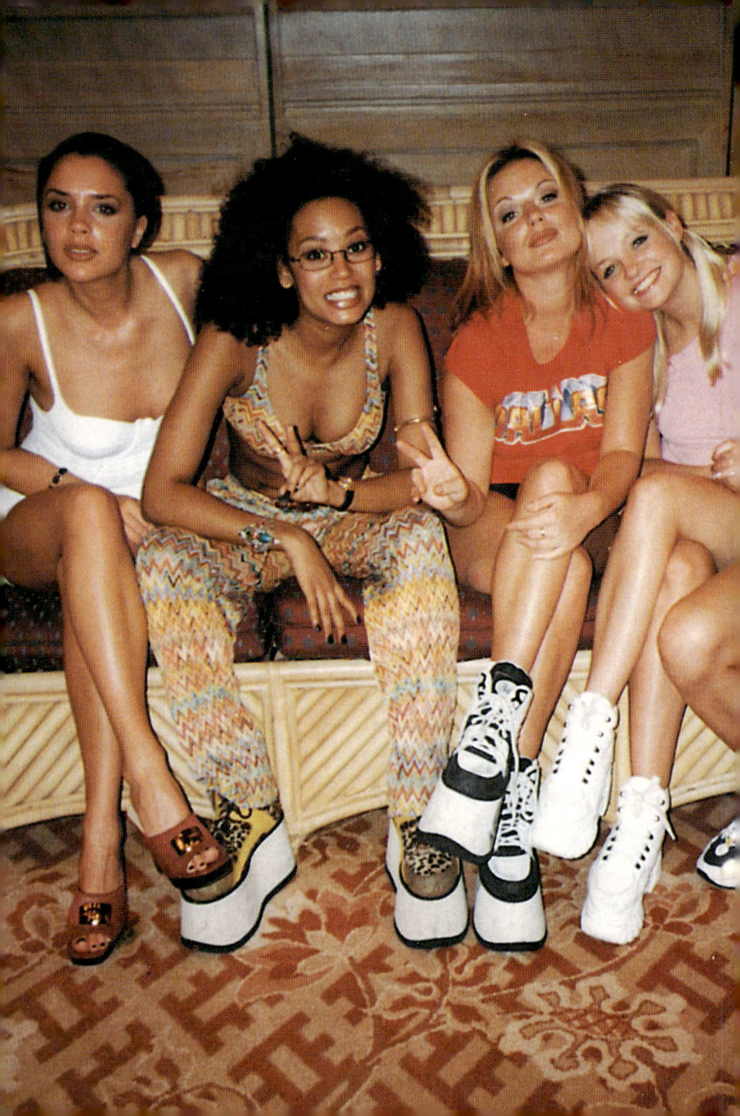

"We've got past the annoying stage and beyond the 'you're-really-doing-my-head-in' stage. We get on better now than ever before – we can say anything to each other. A lot of the time we know what the others are thinking, without talking at all."

"Girl Power is about realising that you don't have to stand for any rubbish from anyone especially not from blokes!"

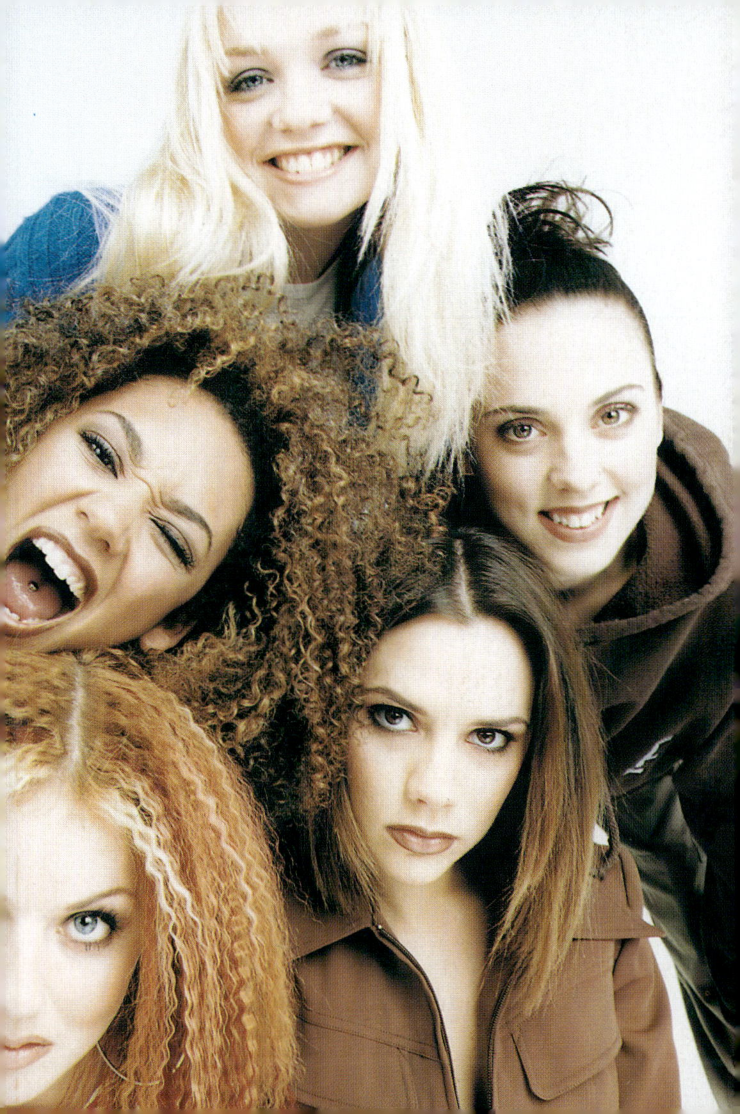

"What's important is the message. There's a colourful element that attracts the younger generation, but then if you want to read between the lines, there is a funny sick sense of humour there and a deeper message – if you want to get it."

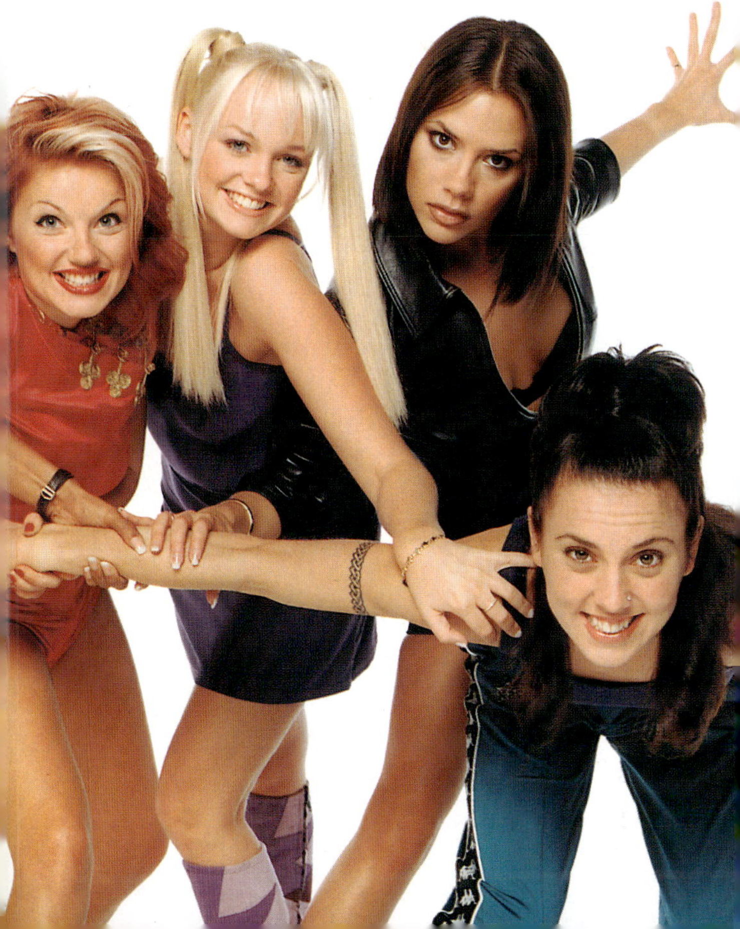

Thanks for reading my book!

GET THE SET! FOUR MORE OFFICIAL MINIBOOKS TO COLLECT

SPICE GIRLS OFFICIAL PUBLICATIONS